I0448419

DEC. 2011

Test Results for Forensic Media Preparation
Tool: Image MASSter Solo-4 Forensics;
Software Version 4.2.63.0

NCJ 235711

John Laub

Director, National Institute of Justice

This report was prepared for the National Institute of Justice, U.S. Department of Justice, by the Office of Law Enforcement Standards of the National Institute of Standards and Technology under Interagency Agreement 2003–IJ–R–029.

The National Institute of Justice is a component of the Office of Justice Programs, which also includes the Bureau of Justice Assistance, the Bureau of Justice Statistics, the Office of Juvenile Justice and Delinquency Prevention, and the Office for Victims of Crime.

December 2010

Test Results for Forensic Media Preparation Tool:

Image MASSter Solo-4 Forensics; Software Version 4.2.63.0

**National Institute of
Standards and Technology**
U.S. Department of Commerce

Contents

Introduction 1

How to Read This Report 1

1. Results Summary 3

2. Test Case Selection 4

3. Test Materials 5

    3.1   Support Software 5

    3.2   Test Drive Creation 5

    3.3   Test Drive Analysis 6

    3.4   Test Drives 6

4. Test Results 7

    4.1   Test Results Report Key 7

    4.2   Test Details 8

        4.2.1   FMP-01-ATA28 8

        4.2.2   FMP-01-ATA48 9

        4.2.3   FMP-01-SATA28 10

        4.2.4   FMP-01-SATA48 12

        4.2.5   FMP-01-USB 13

        4.2.6   FMP-02-ATA28 14

        4.2.7   FMP-02-ATA48 15

        4.2.8   FMP-02-SATA28 16

        4.2.9   FMP-02-SATA48 17

        4.2.10   FMP-03-DCO 18

        4.2.11   FMP-03-DCO-2 19

        4.2.12   FMP-03-DCO-HPA 21

        4.2.13   FMP-03-HPA 22

        4.2.14   FMP-04-DCO 23

        4.2.15   FMP-04-DCO-HPA 26

        4.2.16   FMP-04-HPA 27

        4.2.17   FMP-05 28

Introduction

The Computer Forensics Tool Testing (CFTT) program is a joint project of the National Institute of Justice (NIJ), the U.S. Department of Homeland Security (DHS), and the National Institute of Standards and Technology Office of Law Enforcement Standards (OLES) and Information Technology Laboratory (ITL). CFTT is supported by other organizations, including the Federal Bureau of Investigation, the U.S. Department of Defense Cyber Crime Center, U.S. Internal Revenue Service Criminal Investigation Division Electronic Crimes Program, and DHS's Bureau of Immigration and Customs Enforcement, U.S. Customs and Border Protection and U.S. Secret Service. The objective of the CFTT program is to provide measurable assurance to practitioners, researchers and other applicable users that the tools used in computer forensics investigations provide accurate results. Accomplishing this requires the development of specifications and test methods for computer forensics tools and subsequent testing of specific tools against those specifications.

Test results provide the information necessary for developers to improve tools, users to make informed choices, and the legal community and others to understand the tools' capabilities. The CFTT approach to testing computer forensic tools is based on well-recognized methodologies for conformance and quality testing. The specifications and test methods are posted on the CFTT Web site (http://www.cftt.nist.gov/) for review and comment by the computer forensics community.

This document reports the results from testing the wipeout function of Image MASSter Solo-4 Forensics using Software Version 4.2.63.0, against the *Forensic Media Preparation Tool Test Assertions and Test Plan Version 1.0* available at the CFTT Web site (http://www.cftt.nist.gov/fmp-atp-pc-01.pdf).

Test results for other devices and software packages using the CFTT tool methodology can be found on NIJ's computer forensics tool testing Web page, http://www.nij.gov/nij/topics/forensics/evidence/digital/standards/cftt.htm.

How to Read This Report

This report is divided into four sections. The first section is a summary of the results from the test runs. This section is sufficient for most readers to assess the suitability of the tool for the intended use. The remaining sections of the report describe how the tests were conducted and provide documentation of test case details that support the report summary. Section 2 gives the selection of each test case from the set of possible cases defined in the test plan for forensic media preparation tools. The test cases are selected, in general, based on features offered by the tool. Section 3 lists hardware and software used to run the test cases with links to additional information about the items used. Section 4 contains a description of each test case listing all test assertions that apply, the expected result and the actual result. Please refer to the vendor's owner manual for guidance on using the tool.

Test Results for Forensic Media Preparation Tool

Tool Tested:	Image MASSter Solo-4 Forensics
Version:	4.2.63.0
Serial No.	350280
Run Environments:	Custom
Supplier:	Intelligent Computer Solutions, Inc
	9350 Eton Ave.
	Chatsworth, CA 91311
	USA
Tel:	(888) 994-4678
	(818) 998-5805
Fax:	(818) 998-3190
WWW:	http://www.ics-iq.com/index.cfm

1. Results Summary

The Image MASSter Solo-4 Forensics is a multifunctional forensics hand-held disk duplicator. It supports disk wiping on drives attached to the *Evidence Collecting* interface. The wipeout function supports three modes for executing a drive wipe: single pass, full Department of Defense (DoD) Sanitization, and secure erase.

The following anomalies were observed for the Image MASSter Solo-4:

- For one particular hard drive model used in testing, Seagate ST3160815AS, the Solo-4 device halted after drive identification and did not erase any sectors. (Test case FMP-02-SATA48.)
- The Solo-4 did not handle drives correctly if there was a Device Configuration Overlay (DCO) present on the test drive. The following three behaviors were observed:
    - Test Case FMP-03-DCO: The DCO was not erased and the 48 visible sectors immediately preceding the DCO also were not erased. However, the remaining visible sectors were erased.
    - Test case FMP-03-DCO2: The last sector of the DCO was not erased. All other sectors, both hidden and visible, were erased.
    - Test cases FMP-03-DCO-HPA and FMP-04-DCO-HPA: The sectors in the DCO were not erased. All visible sectors and all sectors in the Host Protected Area (HPA) were erased.

The following table provides a quick overview of the test case results:

Test Case	First Sector Overwritten	Last Sector Overwritten	Unchanged Sectors	
			First	Last
FMP-01-ATA28	0	156301487		
FMP-01-ATA48	0	488397167		
FMP-01-SATA28	0	78140159		
FMP-01-SATA48	0	312581807		
FMP-01-USB	0	488397167		
FMP-02-ATA28	0	156301487		
FMP-02-ATA48	0	490234751		
FMP-02-SATA28	0	156301487		
FMP-02-SATA48	n/a	n/a	0	312581807
FMP-03-DCO	0	146301439	146301440	156301487
FMP-03-DCO-2	0	156301486	156301487	156301487
FMP-03-HPA	0	390721967		
FMP-03-DCO-HPA	0	478397167	478397168	488397167
FMP-04-DCO	0	976773167		
FMP-04-DCO-HPA	0	380721967	380721968	390721967
FMP-04-HPA	0	234441647		
FMP-05	NA	NA	NA	

2. Test Case Selection

The Image MASSter Solo-4 Forensics was only tested for its ability to overwrite sectors of disk drives attached to the *Evidence Collection* interface. The device supports three wipe modes: (1) a User mode that overwrites target drives using the ATA WRITE command, (2) a Secure Erase mode where the device issues the ATA SECURITY ERASE command and (3) a multi-pass DoD wipe command.

The test cases were selected from cases defined by *Forensic Media Preparation Tool Test Assertions and Test Plan Version 1.0* based on features supported by this tool.

The following wipeout modes were selected in testing.

Test Case	Mode
FMP-01-ATA28	User
FMP-01-ATA48	DoD
FMP-01-SATA28	User
FMP-01-SATA48	DoD
FMP-01-USB	User
FMP-02-ATA28	Secure Erase
FMP-02-ATA48	Secure Erase
FMP-02-SATA28	Secure Erase
FMP-02-SATA48	Secure Erase
FMP-03-DCO	User
FMP-03-DCO-2	User

FMP-03-DCO-HPA	User
FMP-03-HPA	DoD
FMP-04-DCO	Secure Erase
FMP-04-DCO-HPA	Secure Erase
FMP-04-HPA	Secure Erase
FMP-05	Secure Erase

The following source interfaces were used in testing: USB, ATA28, ATA48, SATA28, and SATA48.

3. Test Materials

3.1 Support Software

Several programs were used in the setup and analysis of the test drives. These include **hdat2** (download from: http://www.hdat2.com/download.html), **dsumm** (download from: http://www.cftt.nist.gov/), **ransum** (download from: http://www.cftt.nist.gov/), and **diskwipe** from **FS-TST Release 2.0** (download from: http://www.cftt.nist.gov/diskimaging/fs-tst20.zip).

The **hdat2** program is used to create, remove and document hidden areas on a drive.

The **dsumm** program analyzes the content of a hard drive. It produces a summary of disk contents in terms of counts for each byte value present on the drive. For example, if a drive can contain 10GB (19531250 sectors of 512 bytes per sector) and the drive is wiped with zero bytes, then **dsumm** reports 10,000,000,000 zero bytes. The program also prints the first sector found with printable ASCII content.

The **ransum** program examines a hard drive to identify sectors that do not contain the content written to the drive by the **diskwipe** program. The **ransum** output is a list of sector ranges classified as either *overwritten* or *unchanged*.

The **diskwipe** program initializes a hard drive with known content.

3.2 Test Drive Creation

The following steps are used to setup a test drive:

1. The drive is initially filled with known content by the **diskwipe** program from FS-TST. The **diskwipe** program writes the sector address to each sector in both C/H/S and LBA format. The remainder of the sector bytes are set to a constant fill value unique for each drive. The fill value is noted in the **diskwipe** tool log file.
2. The **dsumm** program analyzes the drive contents. This documents the content of the drive. Each sector has unique content after the setup.

3. If the drive is intended for hidden area tests (FMP-03, FMP-04), an HPA, a DCO or DCO+HPA are created.
4. The drive size after creation of a hidden area is recorded.

3.3 Test Drive Analysis

The following steps are used to analyze a test drive after it has been wiped by the tool under test:

The size of the drive is recorded. This determines if the tool changes the size of a hidden area.
Any hidden areas still remaining on the drive are removed.
The **dsumm** program is run to determine the final content of the drive.
The **ransum** program is run to classify sectors as either *overwritten* or *unchanged*.

3.4 Test Drives

The following hard drives were used in testing. The column labeled **Test Case** identifies the test case. The fill value written by **diskwipe** to initialize the drive is reported in the column labeled **Target Fill**. The column labeled **Sectors** is the size of the drive with no DCO or HPA. The column labeled **Model** is the model of the drive as returned by the ATA IDENTIFY DEVICE command. The column labeled **Serial #** is the serial number as returned by the ATA IDENTIFY DEVICE command.

Test Case	Target Fill (hex value)	Sectors	Model	Serial #
FMP-01-ATA28	0xFF	156301488	WDC WD800BB-75CAA0	WD-WMA8E2108916
FMP-01-ATA48	0xF6	488397168	WDC WD2500JB-00GVC0	WD-WCAL78188039
FMP-01-SATA28	0x5A	78140160	FUJITSU MHW2040BH	K10XT7B278AP
FMP-01-SATA48	0x90	312581808	ST3160815AS	9RX7Y1DP
FMP-01-USB	0xFF	488397168	WD2500JB-00FUA0	
FMP-02-ATA28	0x00	156301488	Hitachi HTS541680J9AT00	SB0241HGGAWN9E
FMP-02-ATA48	0x00	490234752	Maxtor 7Y250P0	Y63FSHTE
FMP-02-SATA28	0x00	156301488	Hitachi HDS721680PLA380	PVF804Z31NKPSN
FMP-02-SATA48	0x00	312581808	ST3160815AS	9RX7Y1DP
FMP-03-DCO	0x00	156301488	FUJITSU MHW2080AT	K004T832CK2R
FMP-03-DCO-2	0xFF	156301488	Hitachi HTS541680J9AT00	SB0241HGGAWN9E
FMP-03-HPA	0xF6	390721968	TOSHIBA MK2049GSY	788DT0FLT
FMP-03-DCO-HPA	0xFF	488397168	WDC WD2500JB-00GVC0	WD-WCAL78188039
FMP-04-DCO	0x00	976773168	SAMSUNG HM500LI	S1HMJD0Q908367
FMP-04-DCO-HPA	0x00	390721968	TOSHIBA MK2049GSY	788DT0FLT
FMP-04-HPA	0x00	234441648	WDC WD1200JD-00GBB0	WD-WMAES2049679
FMP-05	NA	156301488	WDC WD800BB-75CAA0	WD-WMA8E2108916

The table that follows lists the drive configurations for hidden sector test cases. The column labeled **Test Case** identifies the test case. The column labeled **Size** is the number of visible sectors presented to the device for the test case. The size of the drive including both visible and hidden sectors is reported in the column labeled **Total**. The column labeled **Hidden** is the size in sectors of the hidden area.

Test Case	Size	Total	Hidden (DCO+HPA)
FMP-03-DCO	146301488	156301488	10000000
FMP-03-DCO-2	146301488	156301488	10000000
FMP-03-DCO-HPA	463397168	488397168	25000000 (10000000+15000000)
FMP-03-HPA	15000001	390721968	15000000
FMP-04-DCO	966773168	976773168	10000000
FMP-04-DCO-HPA	365721968	390721968	25000000 (10000000+15000000)
FMP-04-HPA	375721968	390721968	15000000

4. Test Results

The main item of interest for interpreting the test results is determining the conformance of the tool under test with the test assertions. Conformance with each assertion tested by a given test case is evaluated by examining the **Log Highlights** box of the test report details.

4.1 Test Results Report Key

A summary of the actual test results is presented in this report. The following table presents a description of each section of the test report summary.

Heading	Description
First Line:	Test case ID, name and version of tool tested.
Case Summary:	Test case summary from *Forensic Media Preparation Tool Test Assertions and Test Plan Version 1.0*.
Assertions:	The test assertions applicable to the test case, selected from *Forensic Media Preparation Tool Test Assertions and Test Plan Version 1.0*.
Tester Name:	Name or initials of person executing test procedure.
Analysis Host:	Host used to setup test drive and analyze final drive state.
Test Host:	Host computer executing the test.
Test Date:	Time and date that test was started.
Test Drive:	Drive erased by the tool under test.
Source Setup:	Report of the native drive size, the size of any hidden areas, the apparent size of the drive (as reported by an ATA IDENTIFY DEVICE command) and an analysis of initial drive contents.
Tool Settings:	Report of tool parameters set for each test run.
Log Highlights:	Report of the state of the drive after executing the tool under test, including the apparent drive size, size of hidden area and analysis of drive contents. The ASCII content of the first non-binary-zero sector is reported.
Results:	Expected and actual results for each assertion tested.
Analysis:	Whether or not the expected results were achieved.

4.2 Test Details

4.2.1 FMP-01-ATA28

Test Case FMP-01-ATA28 Image MASSter Solo-4 version 4.2.63.0	
Case Summary:	FMP-01. Overwrite visible sectors using WRITE commands.
Assertions:	FMP-CA-01 All visible sectors shall be overwritten with the specified benign data.
Tester Name:	csr
Analysis host:	frank
Test host:	none
Test date:	Thu Jul 8 12:03:08 2010
Test drive:	56-IDE

Source Setup:	Initial setup size: 156301488 from total of 156301488 (with 0 hidden) IDE disk: Model (WDC WD800BB-75CAA0) serial # (WD-WMA8E2108916)
	
	Sector 0 is first sector with printable text
	============== Start text ==============
	00000/000/01 000000000000VVVVVVVVVVVVVVVVVVVVVVVVVVVVVVVVVVVV
	VVVVVVVVVVVVVVVVVVVVVVVVVVVVVVVVVVVVVVVVVVVVVVVVVVVVVVVVVVVVVV
	VVVVVVVVVVVVVVVVVVVVVVVVVVVVVVVVVVVVVVVVVVVVVVVVVVVVVVVVVVVVVV
	VVVVVVVVVVVVVVVVVVVVVVVVVVVVVVVVVVVVVVVVVVVVVVVVVVVVVVVVVVVVVV
	VVVVVVVVVVVVVVVVVVVVVVVVVVVVVVVVVVVVVVVVVVVVVVVVVVVVVVVVVVVVVV
	VVVVVVVVVVVVVVVVVVVVVVVVVVVVVVVVVVVVVVVVVVVVVVVVVVVVVVVVVVVVVV
	VVVVVVVVVVVVVVVVVVVVVVVVVVVVVVVVVVVVVVVVVVVVVVVVVVVVVVVVVVVVVV
	VVVVVVVVVVVVVVVVVVVVVVVVVVVVVVVVVVVVVVVVVVVVVVVVVVVVVVVVVVVVVV
	VVVVVVVVVVVVVVVVVVVVVVVVVVVVVVVVVV
	============== End text Sector 0 ==============
	9 <new line> characters inserted for readability
	
	Totals for all sectors
	summary format: <count> <hex value> <(actual character if printable)> ...
	   156301488 00 156301488 20 ( ) 312602976 2F (/)
	  1092738319 30 (0) 445157427 31 (1) 274740905 32 (2)
	   274642393 33 (3) 272159917 34 (4) 262536293 35 (5)
	   225709546 36 (6) 215483146 37 (7) 215483143 38 (8)
	   215483135 39 (9) 75907021680 56 (V)
	Totals for non-ASCII sectors
	summary format: <count> <hex value> <(actual character if printable)> ...
	
	80026361856 bytes, 156301488 sectors, 14 distinct values seen
	156301488 sectors have printable text

Tool Settings:	Mode: User Iteration: 1 Pattern: 0xFF

Log Highlights:	Size after tool runs: 156301488 from total of 156301488 (with 0 hidden)
	Analysis of tool result --
	Totals for all sectors
	summary format: <count> <hex value> <(actual character if printable)> ...
	  80026361856 FF
	Totals for non-ASCII sectors
	summary format: <count> <hex value> <(actual character if printable)> ...
	  80026361856 FF
	
	80026361856 bytes, 156301488 sectors, 1 distinct values seen
	No sectors have printable text
	
	     Runs of Sectors Unchanged or Overwritten
	First Sector Last Sector State
	          0 -- 156301487 Overwritten

Results:	Assertion & Expected Result	Actual Result	
	FMP-CA-01 Visible sectors overwritten	as expected	
Analysis:	Expected results achieved		

4.2.2 FMP-01-ATA48

Test Case FMP-01-ATA48 Image MASSter Solo-4 version 4.2.63.0	
Case Summary:	FMP-01. Overwrite visible sectors using WRITE commands.
Assertions:	FMP-CA-01 All visible sectors shall be overwritten with the specified benign data.
Tester Name:	csr
Analysis host:	frank
Test host:	none
Test date:	Fri Jul 9 06:46:25 2010
Test drive:	29-IDE

Source Setup:	Initial setup size: 488397168 from total of 488397168 (with 0 hidden)
	IDE disk: Model (WDC WD2500JB-00GVC0) serial # (WD-WCAL78188039)
	
	Sector 0 is first sector with printable text
	============= Start text =============
	00000/000/01 000000000000))))))))))))))))))))))))))))))))))))))
	)))
	)))
	)))
	)))
	)))
	)))
	)))
	))))))))))))))))))))))))))))))))))))
	============= End text Sector 0 =============
	9 <new line> characters inserted for readability
	
	Totals for all sectors
	summary format: <count> <hex value> <(actual character if printable)> ...
	   488397168 00 488397168 20 ( ) 237361023648 29 ())
	   976794336 2F (/) 2735169210 30 (0) 1278997882 31 (1)
	  1192805876 32 (2) 933260747 33 (3) 905775911 34 (4)
	   805865997 35 (5) 749775664 36 (6) 718765480 37 (7)
	   716559080 38 (8) 707761849 39 (9)
	Totals for non-ASCII sectors
	summary format: <count> <hex value> <(actual character if printable)> ...
	
	250059350016 bytes, 488397168 sectors, 14 distinct values seen
	488397168 sectors have printable text

Tool Settings:	Mode: DoD Iteration: 3 Pattern: 0xF6

Log Highlights:	Size after tool runs: 488397168 from total of 488397168 (with 0 hidden)
	Analysis of tool result --
	Totals for all sectors
	summary format: <count> <hex value> <(actual character if printable)> ...
	250059350016 F6
	Totals for non-ASCII sectors
	summary format: <count> <hex value> <(actual character if printable)> ...
	250059350016 F6
	
	250059350016 bytes, 488397168 sectors, 1 distinct values seen
	No sectors have printable text
	
	   Runs of Sectors Unchanged or Overwritten
	First Sector Last Sector State
	      0 -- 488397167 Overwritten

Results:	**Assertion & Expected Result** **Actual Result** FMP-CA-01 Visible sectors overwritten as expected
Analysis:	Expected results achieved

4.2.3 FMP-01-SATA28

Test Case FMP-01-SATA28 Image MASSter Solo-4 version 4.2.63.0	
Case Summary:	FMP-01. Overwrite visible sectors using WRITE commands.
Assertions:	FMP-CA-01 All visible sectors shall be overwritten with the specified benign data.
Tester Name:	csr
Analysis host:	frank
Test host:	none
Test date:	Sat Jul 10 10:27:41 2010
Test drive:	24-LAP
Source Setup:	Initial setup size: 78140160 from total of 78140160 (with 0 hidden) IDE disk: Model (FUJITSU MHW2040BH) serial # (K10XT7B278AP) Sector 0 is first sector with printable text ============= Start text ============= 00000/000/01 000000000000$$$$$$$$$$$$$$$$$$$$$$$$$$$$$$$$$$$$$$$ $$ $$ $$ $$ $$ $$ $$ $$$$$$$$$$$$$$$$$$$$$$$$$$$$$$$$ ============= End text Sector 0 ============= 9 <new line> characters inserted for readability Totals for all sectors summary format: <count> <hex value> <(actual character if printable)> ... 　78140160 00　　　　　　78140160 20 ( )　37976117760 24 ($) 　156280320 2F (/)　　561878293 30 (0)　173598093 31 (1) 　159768433 32 (2)　　142914673 33 (3)　139463608 34 (4) 　123744696 35 (5)　　114674216 36 (6)　107788836 37 (7) 　98210496 38 (8)　　97042176 39 (9) Totals for non-ASCII sectors summary format: <count> <hex value> <(actual character if printable)> ... 40007761920 bytes, 78140160 sectors, 14 distinct values seen 78140160 sectors have printable text
Tool Settings:	Mode: User Iteration: 1 Pattern: 0x90
Log Highlights:	Size after tool runs: 78140160 from total of 78140160 (with 0 hidden) Analysis of tool result -- Totals for all sectors summary format: <count> <hex value> <(actual character if printable)> ... 　40007761920 90 Totals for non-ASCII sectors summary format: <count> <hex value> <(actual character if printable)> ... 　40007761920 90 40007761920 bytes, 78140160 sectors, 1 distinct values seen No sectors have printable text 　　Runs of Sectors Unchanged or Overwritten First Sector　　Last Sector　　State 　　　0 --　　78140159　Overwritten
Results:	**Assertion & Expected Result** / **Actual Result** FMP-CA-01 Visible sectors overwritten / as expected
Analysis:	Expected results achieved

4.2.4 FMP-01-SATA48

Test Case FMP-01-SATA48 Image MASSter Solo-4 version 4.2.63.0	
Case Summary:	FMP-01. Overwrite visible sectors using WRITE commands.
Assertions:	FMP-CA-01 All visible sectors shall be overwritten with the specified benign data.
Tester Name:	csr
Analysis host:	frank
Test host:	none
Test date:	Sun Jul 11 07:26:24 2010
Test drive:	43-SATA

Source Setup:	Initial setup size: 312581808 from total of 312581808 (with 0 hidden)
	IDE disk: Model (ST3160815AS) serial # (9RX7Y1DP)
	
	Sector 0 is first sector with printable text
	============= Start text =============
	00000/000/01 000000000000CCCCCCCCCCCCCCCCCCCCCCCCCCCCCCCCCCCC
	CCCCCCCCCCCCCCCCCCCCCCCCCCCCCCCCCCCCCCCCCCCCCCCCCCCCCCCCCCCCCC
	CCCCCCCCCCCCCCCCCCCCCCCCCCCCCCCCCCCCCCCCCCCCCCCCCCCCCCCCCCCCCC
	CCCCCCCCCCCCCCCCCCCCCCCCCCCCCCCCCCCCCCCCCCCCCCCCCCCCCCCCCCCCCC
	CCCCCCCCCCCCCCCCCCCCCCCCCCCCCCCCCCCCCCCCCCCCCCCCCCCCCCCCCCCCCC
	CCCCCCCCCCCCCCCCCCCCCCCCCCCCCCCCCCCCCCCCCCCCCCCCCCCCCCCCCCCCCC
	CCCCCCCCCCCCCCCCCCCCCCCCCCCCCCCCCCCCCCCCCCCCCCCCCCCCCCCCCCCCCC
	CCCCCCCCCCCCCCCCCCCCCCCCCCCCCCCCCCCCCCCCCCCCCCCCCCCCCCCCCCCCCC
	CCCCCCCCCCCCCCCCCCCCCCCCCCCCCCCCC
	============= End text Sector 0 =============
	9 \<new line\> characters inserted for readability
	
	Totals for all sectors
	summary format: \<count\> \<hex value\> \<(actual character if printable)\> ...
	   312581808 00 312581808 20 ( ) 625163616 2F (/)
	  1850492169 30 (0) 906528227 31 (1) 696435016 32 (2)
	   541016511 33 (3) 522787395 34 (4) 514450557 35 (5)
	   478352540 36 (6) 458495114 37 (7) 458481159 38 (8)
	   449761088 39 (9) 151914758688 43 (C)
	Totals for non-ASCII sectors
	summary format: \<count\> \<hex value\> \<(actual character if printable)\> ...
	
	160041885696 bytes, 312581808 sectors, 14 distinct values seen
	312581808 sectors have printable text

Tool Settings:	Mode: DoD Iteration: 3 Pattern: 0xF6

Log Highlights:	Size after tool runs: 312581808 from total of 312581808 (with 0 hidden)
	Analysis of tool result --
	Totals for all sectors
	summary format: \<count\> \<hex value\> \<(actual character if printable)\> ...
	160041885696 F6
	Totals for non-ASCII sectors
	summary format: \<count\> \<hex value\> \<(actual character if printable)\> ...
	160041885696 F6
	
	160041885696 bytes, 312581808 sectors, 1 distinct values seen
	No sectors have printable text
	
	    Runs of Sectors Unchanged or Overwritten
	First Sector Last Sector State
	     0 -- 312581807 Overwritten

Results:	Assertion & Expected Result / Actual Result FMP-CA-01 Visible sectors overwritten | as expected
Analysis:	Expected results achieved

4.2.5 FMP-01-USB

Test Case FMP-01-USB Image MASSter Solo-4 version 4.2.63.0	
Case Summary:	FMP-01. Overwrite visible sectors using WRITE commands.
Assertions:	FMP-CA-01 All visible sectors shall be overwritten with the specified benign data.
Tester Name:	csr
Analysis host:	frank
Test host:	none
Test date:	Tue Jul 13 06:43:36 2010
Test drive:	2C-FU2

Source Setup:	Initial setup size: 488397168 from total of 488397168 (with 0 hidden)
	Model (WD2500JB-00FUA0) serial # ()
	
	Sector 0 is first sector with printable text
	============== Start text =============
	00000/000/01 000000000000,,,,,,,,,,,,,,,,,,,,,,,,,,,,,,,,,,,,
	,,,
	,,,
	,,,
	,,,
	,,,
	,,,
	,,,
	,,,,,,,,,,,,,,,,,,,,,,,,,,,,,,,,
	============== End text Sector 0 =============
	9 <new line> characters inserted for readability
	
	Totals for all sectors
	summary format: <count> <hex value> <(actual character if printable)> ...
	   488397168 00 488397168 20 ( ) 237361023648 2C (,)
	   976794336 2F (/) 2735169210 30 (0) 1278997882 31 (1)
	  1192805876 32 (2) 933260747 33 (3) 905775911 34 (4)
	   805865997 35 (5) 749775664 36 (6) 718765480 37 (7)
	   716559080 38 (8) 707761849 39 (9)
	Totals for non-ASCII sectors
	summary format: <count> <hex value> <(actual character if printable)> ...
	
	250059350016 bytes, 488397168 sectors, 14 distinct values seen
	488397168 sectors have printable text

Tool Settings:	Mode: User Iteration: 1 Pattern: 0xFF

Log Highlights:	Size after tool runs: 488397168 from total of 488397168 (with 0 hidden)
	Analysis of tool result --
	Totals for all sectors
	summary format: <count> <hex value> <(actual character if printable)> ...
	250059350016 FF
	Totals for non-ASCII sectors
	summary format: <count> <hex value> <(actual character if printable)> ...
	250059350016 FF
	
	250059350016 bytes, 488397168 sectors, 1 distinct values seen
	No sectors have printable text
	
	   Runs of Sectors Unchanged or Overwritten
	First Sector Last Sector State
	      0 -- 488397167 Overwritten

Results:	**Assertion & Expected Result**	**Actual Result**
	FMP-CA-01 Visible sectors overwritten	as expected
Analysis:	Expected results achieved	

4.2.6 FMP-02-ATA28

Test Case FMP-02-ATA28 Image MASSter Solo-4 version 4.2.63.0	
Case Summary:	FMP-02. Overwrite visible sectors using an ERASE command.
Assertions:	FMP-AO-03 If the tool supports overwrite command selection and an ERASE command is selected then all visible sectors are overwritten.
Tester Name:	csr
Analysis host:	frank
Test host:	none
Test date:	Wed Jul 14 09:25:59 2010
Test drive:	14-LAP

Source Setup:	Initial setup size: 156301488 from total of 156301488 (with 0 hidden) IDE disk: Model (Hitachi HTS541680J9AT00) serial # (SB0241HGGAWN9E)
	
	Sector 0 is first sector with printable text
	============= Start text =============
	00000/000/01 000000000000
	============= End text Sector 0 =============
	1 \<new line\> character inserted for readability
	
	Totals for all sectors
	summary format: \<count\> \<hex value\> \<(actual character if printable)\> ...
	  156301488 00 75962523168 14 156301488 20 ( )
	  312602976 2F (/) 1051401436 30 (0) 387451758 31 (1)
	  303557105 32 (2) 269597920 33 (3) 267115444 34 (4)
	  259739282 35 (5) 234788791 36 (6) 223427887 37 (7)
	  222956329 38 (8) 218596784 39 (9)
	Totals for non-ASCII sectors
	summary format: \<count\> \<hex value\> \<(actual character if printable)\> ...
	
	80026361856 bytes, 156301488 sectors, 14 distinct values seen
	156301488 sectors have printable text

Tool Settings:	Mode: Secure Erase Iteration: 1 Pattern: 00

Log Highlights:	Size after tool runs: 156301488 from total of 156301488 (with 0 hidden)
	Analysis of tool result --
	Totals for all sectors
	summary format: \<count\> \<hex value\> \<(actual character if printable)\> ...
	 80026361856 00
	Totals for non-ASCII sectors
	summary format: \<count\> \<hex value\> \<(actual character if printable)\> ...
	 80026361856 00
	
	80026361856 bytes, 156301488 sectors, 1 distinct values seen
	No sectors have printable text
	
	   Runs of Sectors Unchanged or Overwritten
	First Sector Last Sector State
	      0 -- 156301487 Overwritten

Results:	**Assertion & Expected Result** / **Actual Result** FMP-AO-03 Visible sectors erased / as expected
Analysis:	Expected results achieved

4.2.7 FMP-02-ATA48

Test Case FMP-02-ATA48 Image MASSter Solo-4 version 4.2.63.0	
Case Summary:	FMP-02. Overwrite visible sectors using an ERASE command.
Assertions:	FMP-AO-03 If the tool supports overwrite command selection and an ERASE command is selected then all visible sectors are overwritten.
Tester Name:	csr
Analysis host:	frank
Test host:	none
Test date:	Thu Jul 15 06:54:55 2010
Test drive:	2A-IDE

Source Setup:	Initial setup size: 490234752 from total of 490234752 (with 0 hidden)
	 IDE disk: Model (Maxtor 7Y250P0) serial # (Y63FSHTE)
	
	 Sector 0 is first sector with printable text
	 ============= Start text =============
	 00000/000/01 000000000000***********************************
	 **
	 **
	 **
	 **
	 **
	 **
	 **
	 *****************************
	 ============= End text Sector 0 =============
	 9 \<new line\> characters inserted for readability
	
	 Totals for all sectors
	 summary format: \<count\> \<hex value\> \<(actual character if printable)\> ...
	  490234752 00 490234752 20 ( ) 238254089472 2A (*)
	  980469504 2F (/) 2745916670 30 (0) 1282185547 31 (1)
	  1195513694 32 (2) 937373971 33 (3) 911537467 34 (4)
	  808408249 35 (5) 751843469 36 (6) 720717342 37 (7)
	  720716723 38 (8) 710951412 39 (9)
	 Totals for non-ASCII sectors
	 summary format: \<count\> \<hex value\> \<(actual character if printable)\> ...
	
	 251000193024 bytes, 490234752 sectors, 14 distinct values seen
	 490234752 sectors have printable text

Tool Settings:	Mode: Secure Erase Itertion: 1 Pattern: 00

Log Highlights:	Size after tool runs: 490234752 from total of 490234752 (with 0 hidden)
	 Analysis of tool result --
	 Totals for all sectors
	 summary format: \<count\> \<hex value\> \<(actual character if printable)\> ...
	 251000193024 00
	 Totals for non-ASCII sectors
	 summary format: \<count\> \<hex value\> \<(actual character if printable)\> ...
	 251000193024 00
	
	 251000193024 bytes, 490234752 sectors, 1 distinct values seen
	 No sectors have printable text
	
	    Runs of Sectors Unchanged or Overwritten
	 First Sector Last Sector State
	        0 -- 490234751 Overwritten

Results:	**Assertion & Expected Result** / **Actual Result** FMP-AO-03 Visible sectors erased | as expected
Analysis:	Expected results achieved

4.2.8 FMP-02-SATA28

Test Case FMP-02-SATA28 Image MASSter Solo-4 version 4.2.63.0	
Case Summary:	FMP-02. Overwrite visible sectors using an ERASE command.
Assertions:	FMP-AO-03 If the tool supports overwrite command selection and an ERASE command is selected then all visible sectors are overwritten.
Tester Name:	csr
Analysis host:	frank
Test host:	none
Test date:	Thu Jul 15 15:37:17 2010
Test drive:	32-SATA

Source Setup:	Initial setup size: 156301488 from total of 156301488 (with 0 hidden)
	IDE disk: Model (Hitachi HDS721680PLA380) serial # (PVF804Z31NKPSN)
	
	Sector 0 is first sector with printable text
	============= Start text =============
	00000/000/01 00000000000022222222222222222222222222222222222
	22222222222222222222222222222222222222222222222222222222222222
	22222222222222222222222222222222222222222222222222222222222222
	22222222222222222222222222222222222222222222222222222222222222
	22222222222222222222222222222222222222222222222222222222222222
	22222222222222222222222222222222222222222222222222222222222222
	22222222222222222222222222222222222222222222222222222222222222
	22222222222222222222222222222222222222222222222222222222222222
	2222222222222222222222222222222
	============= End text Sector 0 =============
	9 \<new line\> characters inserted for readability
	
	Totals for all sectors
	summary format: \<count\> \<hex value\> \<(actual character if printable)\> ...
	  156301488 00 156301488 20 ( ) 312602976 2F (/)
	 1051401436 30 (0) 387451758 31 (1) 76266080273 32 (2)
	  269597920 33 (3) 267115444 34 (4) 259739282 35 (5)
	  234788791 36 (6) 223427887 37 (7) 222956329 38 (8)
	  218596784 39 (9)
	Totals for non-ASCII sectors
	summary format: \<count\> \<hex value\> \<(actual character if printable)\> ...
	
	80026361856 bytes, 156301488 sectors, 13 distinct values seen
	156301488 sectors have printable text

Tool Settings:	Mode: Secure Erase Iteration: 1 Pattern: 00

Log Highlights:	Size after tool runs: 156301488 from total of 156301488 (with 0 hidden)
	Analysis of tool result --
	Totals for all sectors
	summary format: \<count\> \<hex value\> \<(actual character if printable)\> ...
	 80026361856 00
	Totals for non-ASCII sectors
	summary format: \<count\> \<hex value\> \<(actual character if printable)\> ...
	 80026361856 00
	
	80026361856 bytes, 156301488 sectors, 1 distinct values seen
	No sectors have printable text
	
	     Runs of Sectors Unchanged or Overwritten
	First Sector Last Sector State
	       0 -- 156301487 Overwritten

Results:	**Assertion & Expected Result** **Actual Result**

Test Case FMP-02-SATA28 Image MASSter Solo-4 version 4.2.63.0		
	FMP-AO-03 Visible sectors erased	as expected
Analysis:	Expected results achieved	

4.2.9 FMP-02-SATA48

Test Case FMP-02-SATA48 Image MASSter Solo-4 version 4.2.63.0	
Case Summary:	FMP-02. Overwrite visible sectors using an ERASE command.
Assertions:	FMP-AO-03 If the tool supports overwrite command selection and an ERASE command is selected then all visible sectors are overwritten.
Tester Name:	csr
Analysis host:	frank
Test host:	none
Test date:	Tue Jul 20 11:13:28 2010
Test drive:	43-SATA

Source Setup:	Initial setup size: 312581808 from total of 312581808 (with 0 hidden)
	IDE disk: Model (ST3160815AS) serial # (9RX7Y1DP)
	
	Sector 0 is first sector with printable text
	============= Start text =============
	00000/000/01 000000000000CCCCCCCCCCCCCCCCCCCCCCCCCCCCCCCCCCCCCCC
	CCCCCCCCCCCCCCCCCCCCCCCCCCCCCCCCCCCCCCCCCCCCCCCCCCCCCCCCCCCCCCCCC
	CCCCCCCCCCCCCCCCCCCCCCCCCCCCCCCCCCCCCCCCCCCCCCCCCCCCCCCCCCCCCCCCC
	CCCCCCCCCCCCCCCCCCCCCCCCCCCCCCCCCCCCCCCCCCCCCCCCCCCCCCCCCCCCCCCCC
	CCCCCCCCCCCCCCCCCCCCCCCCCCCCCCCCCCCCCCCCCCCCCCCCCCCCCCCCCCCCCCCCC
	CCCCCCCCCCCCCCCCCCCCCCCCCCCCCCCCCCCCCCCCCCCCCCCCCCCCCCCCCCCCCCCCC
	CCCCCCCCCCCCCCCCCCCCCCCCCCCCCCCCCCCCCCCCCCCCCCCCCCCCCCCCCCCCCCCCC
	CCCCCCCCCCCCCCCCCCCCCCCCCCCCCCCCCCCCCCCCCCCCCCCCCCCCCCCCCCCCCCCCC
	CCCCCCCCCCCCCCCCCCCCCCCCCCCCCCCC
	============= End text Sector 0 =============
	9 <new line> characters inserted for readability
	
	Totals for all sectors
	summary format: <count> <hex value> <(actual character if printable)> ...
	  312581808 00 312581808 20 ( ) 625163616 2F (/)
	  1850492169 30 (0) 906528227 31 (1) 696435016 32 (2)
	  541016511 33 (3) 522787395 34 (4) 514450557 35 (5)
	  478352540 36 (6) 458495114 37 (7) 458481159 38 (8)
	  449761088 39 (9) 151914758688 43 (C)
	Totals for non-ASCII sectors
	summary format: <count> <hex value> <(actual character if printable)> ...
	
	160041885696 bytes, 312581808 sectors, 14 distinct values seen
	312581808 sectors have printable text

Tool Settings:	Mode: Secure Erase Iteration: 1 Pattern: 00
Log Highlights:	Size after tool runs: 312581808 from total of 312581808 (with 0 hidden) Analysis of tool result -- Sector 0 is first sector with printable text ============= Start text ============= 00000/000/01 000000000000CCCCCCCCCCCCCCCCCCCCCCCCCCCCCCCCCCCCCCC CCCCCCCCCCCCCCCCCCCCCCCCCCCCCCCCCCCCCCCCCCCCCCCCCCCCCCCCCCCCCCCCC CCCCCCCCCCCCCCCCCCCCCCCCCCCCCCCCCCCCCCCCCCCCCCCCCCCCCCCCCCCCCCCCC CCCCCCCCCCCCCCCCCCCCCCCCCCCCCCCCCCCCCCCCCCCCCCCCCCCCCCCCCCCCCCCCC CCCCCCCCCCCCCCCCCCCCCCCCCCCCCCCCCCCCCCCCCCCCCCCCCCCCCCCCCCCCCCCCC CCCCCCCCCCCCCCCCCCCCCCCCCCCCCCCCCCCCCCCCCCCCCCCCCCCCCCCCCCCCCCCCC CCCCCCCCCCCCCCCCCCCCCCCCCCCCCCCCCCCCCCCCCCCCCCCCCCCCCCCCCCCCCCCCC CCCCCCCCCCCCCCCCCCCCCCCCCCCCCCCCCCCCCCCCCCCCCCCCCCCCCCCCCCCCCCCCC CCCCCCCCCCCCCCCCCCCCCCCCCCCCCCCC ============= End text Sector 0 =============

Test Case FMP-02-SATA48 Image MASSter Solo-4 version 4.2.63.0	

	9 <new line> characters inserted for readability
	
	Totals for all sectors
	summary format: <count> <hex value> <(actual character if printable)> ...
	   312581808 00 312581808 20 ( ) 625163616 2F (/)
	 1850492169 30 (0) 906528227 31 (1) 696435016 32 (2)
	  541016511 33 (3) 522787395 34 (4) 514450557 35 (5)
	  478352540 36 (6) 458495114 37 (7) 458481159 38 (8)
	  449761088 39 (9) 151914758688 43 (C)
	Totals for non-ASCII sectors
	summary format: <count> <hex value> <(actual character if printable)> ...
	
	160041885696 bytes, 312581808 sectors, 14 distinct values seen
	312581808 sectors have printable text
	
	    Runs of Sectors Unchanged or Overwritten
	First Sector Last Sector State
	      0 -- 312581807 Unchanged

Results:	Assertion & Expected Result	Actual Result	
	FMP-AO-03 Visible sectors erased	No sectors erased	
Analysis:	Expected results not achieved		

4.2.10   FMP-03-DCO

Test Case FMP-03-DCO Image MASSter Solo-4 version 4.2.63.0	
Case Summary:	FMP-03. Overwrite hidden sectors using WRITE commands.
Assertions:	FMP-CA-01 All visible sectors shall be overwritten with the specified benign data. FMP-AO-01 If there is a hidden area present and the tool supports overwriting sectors contained in a hidden area, then all sectors contained in the hidden area shall be overwritten with the specified benign data. FMP-AO-02 A hidden area may optionally be removed from the storage device.
Tester Name:	csr
Analysis host:	frank
Test host:	none
Test date:	Tue Jul 20 07:33:14 2010
Test drive:	19-LAP

Source Setup:	Size with DCO: 146301488 74.91 GB (10000000 sectors in DCO)
	Initial setup size: 146301488 from total of 156301488 (with 10000000 hidden)
	IDE disk: Model (FUJITSU MHW2080AT) serial # (K004T832CK2R)
	
	Sector 0 is first sector with printable text
	============= Start text =============
	00000/000/01 000000000000
	============= End text Sector 0 =============
	1 <new line> character inserted for readability
	
	Totals for all sectors
	summary format: <count> <hex value> <(actual character if printable)> ...
	  146301488 00 71057021680 19 146301488 20 ( )
	  292602976 2F (/) 1031882339 30 (0) 406485727 31 (1)
	  259778655 32 (2) 259680143 33 (3) 248749661 34 (4)
	  236399701 35 (5) 212482354 36 (6) 202891886 37 (7)
	  202891883 38 (8) 202891875 39 (9)
	Totals for non-ASCII sectors
	summary format: <count> <hex value> <(actual character if printable)> ...
	
	74906361856 bytes, 146301488 sectors, 14 distinct values seen
	146301488 sectors have printable text

Tool	Mode: User

Test Case FMP-03-DCO Image MASSter Solo-4 version 4.2.63.0	
Settings:	Iteration: 1 Pattern: 00

Log
Highlights:
	Size after tool runs: 156301488 from total of 156301488 (with 0 hidden)
	Analysis of tool result --
	
	Sector 146301440 is first sector with printable text
	============= Start text =============
	145140/005/06 000146301440
	============= End text Sector 146301440 =============
	1 \<new line\> character inserted for readability
	
	Totals for all sectors
	summary format: \<count\> \<hex value\> \<(actual character if printable)\> ...
	 74916337328 00 4850023280 19 10000048 20 ( )
	   20000096 2F (/) 60856330 30 (0) 38671912 31 (1)
	   14962270 32 (2) 14962318 33 (3) 23410477 34 (4)
	   26136711 35 (5) 13227260 36 (6) 12591280 37 (7)
	   12591277 38 (8) 12591269 39 (9)
	Totals for non-ASCII sectors
	summary format: \<count\> \<hex value\> \<(actual character if printable)\> ...
	 74906337280 00
	
	80026361856 bytes, 156301488 sectors, 14 distinct values seen
	10000048 sectors have printable text
	
	    Runs of Sectors Unchanged or Overwritten
	First Sector Last Sector State
	          0 -- 146301439 Overwritten
	  146301440 -- 156301487 Unchanged

Results:	Assertion & Expected Result	Actual Result	
	FMP-CA-01 Visible sectors overwritten	as expected	
	FMP-AO-01 Hidden sectors overwritten	DCO not overwritten	
	FMP-AO-02 Hidden area final state is	removed	
Analysis:	Expected results not achieved		

4.2.11   FMP-03-DCO-2

Test Case FMP-03-DCO-2 Image MASSter Solo-4 version 4.2.63.0	
Case Summary:	FMP-03. Overwrite hidden sectors using WRITE commands.
Assertions:	FMP-CA-01 All visible sectors shall be overwritten with the specified benign data. FMP-AO-01 If there is a hidden area present and the tool supports overwriting sectors contained in a hidden area, then all sectors contained in the hidden area shall be overwritten with the specified benign data. FMP-AO-02 A hidden area may optionally be removed from the storage device.
Tester Name:	csr
Analysis host:	frank
Test host:	none
Test date:	Sat Oct 16 10:24:37 2010
Test drive:	14-LAP
Source Setup:	Size with DCO: 146301488 74.91 GB (10000000 sectors in DCO) Initial setup size: 146301488 from total of 156301488 (with 10000000 hidden) IDE disk: Model (Hitachi HTS541680J9AT00) serial # (SB0241HGGAWN9E) Sector 0 is first sector with printable text ============= Start text ============= 00000/000/01 000000000000 ============= End text Sector 0 ============= 1 \<new line\> character inserted for readability Totals for all sectors

	summary format: \<count\> \<hex value\> \<(actual character if printable)\> ...
	   146301488 00 71102523168 14 146301488 20 ( )
	   292602976 2F (/) 993890325 30 (0) 358021591 31 (1)
	   285788447 32 (2) 254136647 33 (3) 248114389 34 (4)
	   238370729 35 (5) 220867833 36 (6) 211263767 37 (7)
	   211263764 38 (8) 196915244 39 (9)
	Totals for non-ASCII sectors
	summary format: \<count\> \<hex value\> \<(actual character if printable)\> ...
	
	74906361856 bytes, 146301488 sectors, 14 distinct values seen
	146301488 sectors have printable text

Tool Settings:	Mode: User Iteration: 1 Pattern: FF

Log
Highlights:
	Size after tool runs: 156301488 from total of 156301488 (with 0 hidden)
	Analysis of tool result --
	
	Sector 156301487 is first sector with printable text
	============= Start text =============
	09729/080/63 000156301487
	============= End text Sector 156301487 =============
	1 \<new line\> character inserted for readability
	
	Totals for all sectors
	summary format: \<count\> \<hex value\> \<(actual character if printable)\> ...
	     1 00 486 14 1 20 ( )
	     2 2F (/) 7 30 (0) 2 31 (1)
	     1 32 (2) 2 33 (3) 1 34 (4)
	     1 35 (5) 2 36 (6) 2 37 (7)
	     2 38 (8) 2 39 (9) 80026361344 FF
	Totals for non-ASCII sectors
	summary format: \<count\> \<hex value\> \<(actual character if printable)\> ...
	 80026361344 FF
	
	80026361856 bytes, 156301488 sectors, 15 distinct values seen
	1 sector has printable text
	
	   Runs of Sectors Unchanged or Overwritten
	First Sector Last Sector State
	        0 -- 156301486 Overwritten
	 156301487 -- 156301487 Unchanged

Results:	Assertion & Expected Result	Actual Result	
	FMP-CA-01 Visible sectors overwritten	as expected	
	FMP-AO-01 Hidden sectors overwritten	Last sector of DCO not erased	
	FMP-AO-02 Hidden area final state is	removed	
Analysis:	Expected results not achieved		

4.2.12   FMP-03-DCO-HPA

Test Case FMP-03-DCO-HPA Image MASSter Solo-4 version 4.2.63.0	
Case Summary:	FMP-03. Overwrite hidden sectors using WRITE commands.
Assertions:	FMP-CA-01 All visible sectors shall be overwritten with the specified benign data. FMP-AO-01 If there is a hidden area present and the tool supports overwriting sectors contained in a hidden area, then all sectors contained in the hidden area shall be overwritten with the specified benign data. FMP-AO-02 A hidden area may optionally be removed from the storage device.
Tester Name:	csr
Analysis host:	frank
Test host:	none
Test date:	Thu Aug 19 13:17:57 2010
Test drive:	29-IDE

Source Setup:	Size with DCO: 478397168 244.94 GB (10000000 sectors in DCO)
	Initial setup size: 463397168 from total of 488397168 (with 25000000 hidden)
	IDE disk: Model (WDC WD2500JB-00GVC0) serial # (WD-WCAL78188039)
	
	Sector 0 is first sector with printable text
	============= Start text =============
	00000/000/01 000000000000))))))))))))))))))))))))))))))))))))
	))
	))
	))
	))
	))
	))
	))
	)))))))))))))))))))))))))))))))))))
	============= End text Sector 0 =============
	9 <new line> characters inserted for readability
	
	Totals for all sectors
	summary format: <count> <hex value> <(actual character if printable)> ...
	  478397168 00 478397168 20 ( ) 232501023648 29 ())
	  956794336 2F (/) 2679617860 30 (0) 1259613274 31 (1)
	 1171634074 32 (2) 911352306 33 (3) 882058700 34 (4)
	  792405432 35 (5) 737463673 36 (6) 705127217 37 (7)
	  694715795 38 (8) 690749365 39 (9)
	Totals for non-ASCII sectors
	summary format: <count> <hex value> <(actual character if printable)> ...
	
	244939350016 bytes, 478397168 sectors, 14 distinct values seen
	478397168 sectors have printable text

Tool Settings:	Mode: User Iteration: 1 Pattern: 0xFF
Log Highlights:	Size after tool runs: 478397168 from total of 488397168 (with 10000000 hidden) Analysis of tool result -- Sector 478397168 is first sector with printable text ============= Start text ============= 29778/215/54 000478397168)))))))))))))))))))))))))))))))))))))))))))))))))))))))))))))))))))))))))))))))))))))

Test Case FMP-03-DCO-HPA Image MASSter Solo-4 version 4.2.63.0	

	============= End text Sector 478397168 =============
	9 <new line> characters inserted for readability
	
	Totals for all sectors
	summary format: <count> <hex value> <(actual character if printable)> ...
	244949350016 00 10000000 20 ( ) 4860000000 29 ())
	    20000000 2F (/) 55551350 30 (0) 19384608 31 (1)
	    21171802 32 (2) 21908441 33 (3) 23717211 34 (4)
	    13460565 35 (5) 12311991 36 (6) 13638263 37 (7)
	    21843285 38 (8) 17012484 39 (9)
	Totals for non-ASCII sectors
	summary format: <count> <hex value> <(actual character if printable)> ...
	244939350016 00
	
	250059350016 bytes, 488397168 sectors, 14 distinct values seen
	10000000 sectors have printable text
	
	    Runs of Sectors Unchanged or Overwritten
	First Sector Last Sector State
	          0 -- 478397167 Overwritten
	  478397168 -- 488397167 Unchanged

Results:	Assertion & Expected Result	Actual Result
	FMP-CA-01 Visible sectors overwritten	as expected
	FMP-AO-01 Hidden sectors overwritten	DCO not overwritten
	FMP-AO-02 Hidden area final state is	resized (478397168 with 10000000 hidden)

Analysis:	Expected results not achieved

4.2.13 FMP-03-HPA

Test Case FMP-03-HPA Image MASSter Solo-4 version 4.2.63.0	
Case Summary:	FMP-03. Overwrite hidden sectors using WRITE commands.
Assertions:	FMP-CA-01 All visible sectors shall be overwritten with the specified benign data. FMP-AO-01 If there is a hidden area present and the tool supports overwriting sectors contained in a hidden area, then all sectors contained in the hidden area shall be overwritten with the specified benign data. FMP-AO-02 A hidden area may optionally be removed from the storage device.
Tester Name:	csr
Analysis host:	frank
Test host:	none
Test date:	Thu Jul 22 12:58:50 2010
Test drive:	26-LAP
Source Setup:	Size with HPA: 15000001 7.68 GB (375721967 sectors in HPA) Initial setup size: 15000001 from total of 390721968 (with 375721967 hidden) IDE disk: Model (TOSHIBA MK2049GSY) serial # (788DT0FLT) Sector 0 is first sector with printable text ============= Start text ============= 00000/000/01 000000000000&&&&&&&&&&&&&&&&&&&&&&&&&&&&&&& &&&&&&&&&&&&&&&&&&&&&&&&&&&&&&&&&&&&&&&&&&&&&&&&&&&&&&&&& &&&&&&&&&&&&&&&&&&&&&&&&&&&&&&&&&&&&&&&&&&&&&&&&&&&&&&&&& &&&&&&&&&&&&&&&&&&&&&&&&&&&&&&&&&&&&&&&&&&&&&&&&&&&&&&&&& &&&&&&&&&&&&&&&&&&&&&&&&&&&&&&&&&&&&&&&&&&&&&&&&&&&&&&&&& &&&&&&&&&&&&&&&&&&&&&&&&&&&&&&&&&&&&&&&&&&&&&&&&&&&&&&&&& &&&&&&&&&&&&&&&&&&&&&&&&&&&&&&&&&&&&&&&&&&&&&&&&&&&&&&&&& &&&&&&&&&&&&&&&&&&&&&&&&&&&&&&&&&&&&&&&&&&&&&&&&&&&&&&&&& &&&&&&&&&&&&&&&&&&&&&&&&&&&&& ============= End text Sector 0 ============= 9 <new line> characters inserted for readability

	Test Case FMP-03-HPA Image MASSter Solo-4 version 4.2.63.0

	Totals for all sectors
	summary format: <count> <hex value> <(actual character if printable)> ...
	  390721968 00 390721968 20 ( ) 189890876448 26 (&)
	  781443936 2F (/) 2245711842 30 (0) 1085211682 31 (1)
	  924880030 32 (2) 760620597 33 (3) 652451193 34 (4)
	  638095887 35 (5) 593223154 36 (6) 568337370 37 (7)
	  568314834 38 (8) 559036707 39 (9)
	Totals for non-ASCII sectors
	summary format: <count> <hex value> <(actual character if printable)> ...
	
	200049647616 bytes, 390721968 sectors, 14 distinct values seen
	390721968 sectors have printable text

Tool Settings:	Mode: DoD Iteration: 1 Pattern: F6

Log Highlights:	Size after tool runs: 390721968 from total of 390721968 (with 0 hidden)
	Analysis of tool result --
	Totals for all sectors
	summary format: <count> <hex value> <(actual character if printable)> ...
	200049647616 F6
	Totals for non-ASCII sectors
	summary format: <count> <hex value> <(actual character if printable)> ...
	200049647616 F6
	
	200049647616 bytes, 390721968 sectors, 1 distinct values seen
	No sectors have printable text
	
	  Runs of Sectors Unchanged or Overwritten
	First Sector Last Sector State
	       0 -- 390721967 Overwritten

Results:	<table><tr><td>**Assertion & Expected Result**</td><td>**Actual Result**</td></tr><tr><td>FMP-CA-01 Visible sectors overwritten</td><td>as expected</td></tr><tr><td>FMP-AO-01 Hidden sectors overwritten</td><td>as expected</td></tr><tr><td>FMP-AO-02 Hidden area final state is</td><td>removed</td></tr></table>
Analysis:	Expected results achieved

4.2.14 FMP-04-DCO

	Test Case FMP-04-DCO Image MASSter Solo-4 version 4.2.63.0
Case Summary:	FMP-04. Overwrite hidden sectors using an ERASE command.
Assertions:	FMP-AO-01 If there is a hidden area present and the tool supports overwriting sectors contained in a hidden area, then all sectors contained in the hidden area shall be overwritten with the specified benign data. FMP-AO-02 A hidden area may optionally be removed from the storage device. FMP-AO-03 If the tool supports overwrite command selection and an ERASE command is selected then all visible sectors are overwritten.
Tester Name:	csr
Analysis host:	frank
Test host:	none
Test date:	Wed Oct 6 07:19:27 2010
Test drive:	28-LAP
Source Setup:	Size with DCO: 966773168 494.99 GB (10000000 sectors in DCO) Initial setup size: 966773168 from total of 976773168 (with 10000000 hidden) IDE disk: Model (SAMSUNG HM500LI) serial # (S1HMJD0Q908367) Sector 0 is first sector with printable text ============= Start text ============= 00000/000/01 000000000000(((((((((((((((((((((((((((((((((((

```
((((((((((((((((((((((((((((((((((((((((((((((((((((((((((((((((((((((
((((((((((((((((((((((((((((((((((((((((((((((((((((((((((((((((((((((
((((((((((((((((((((((((((((((((((((((((((((((((((((((((((((((((((((((
((((((((((((((((((((((((((((((((((((((((((((((((((((((((((((((((((((((
((((((((((((((((((((((((((((((((((((((((((((((((((((((((((((((((((((((
((((((((((((((((((((((((((((((((((((((((((((((((((((((((((((((((((((((
((((((((((((((((((((((((((((((((((((((((((((((((((((((((((((((((((((((
((((((((((((((((((((((((((((((((((
============= End text Sector 0 =============
9 <new line> characters inserted for readability

Totals for all sectors
summary format: <count> <hex value> <(actual character if printable)> ...
     966773168 00            966773168 20 ( ) 469851759648 28 (()
    1933546336 2F (/)       5150332728 30 (0)  2277491142 31 (1)
    2105614106 32 (2)       1897095506 33 (3)  1881749732 34 (4)
    1859002432 35 (5)       1586742177 36 (6)  1514888049 37 (7)
    1514667127 38 (8)       1481426697 39 (9)
Totals for non-ASCII sectors
summary format: <count> <hex value> <(actual character if printable)> ...

494987862016 bytes, 966773168 sectors, 14 distinct values seen
966773168 sectors have printable text
```

Tool Settings:	Mode: Secure Erase Iteration: 1 Pattern: 00
Log Highlights:	Size after tool runs: 976773168 from total of 976773168 (with 0 hidden) Analysis of tool result --

```
Sector 512 is first sector with printable text
============= Start text =============

w\_vtV]}z*TQVv$E&U_V]L*TAc6W*o]0qp:>!*]PwDTE_:eU*mUWE|.QMEa:
*k]esUUB8wU.(]E_UP*P&;*tU(UA,Wc uMUUVVU*u.U0E*]U"QWPxE*UUWXn
 RQEU
U{bd&Q}X
}Ez]%+(R9"FmTo"Up$UYu]TAU]a E"*A:"tU*UuUUtVuU3T$Ejb7TSuU:
gU_
]U$Q*Xe
uZEBD
============= End text Sector 512 =============
3 <new line> characters inserted for readability

Totals for all sectors
summary format: <count> <hex value> <(actual character if printable)> ...
 181429182409 00         1601190170 01      1234382458 02
    464937374 03          746797787 04      2019300027 05
    408977748 06          274644879 07       221499392 08
    511704544 09         3008735560 0A        61083522 0B
     14546924 0C          208721751 0D       100186038 0E
     61922487 0F          866364736 10      2284448700 11
    426932321 12          500997856 13      3175756057 14
   4599386966 15          548861561 16       918557912 17
    361627659 18          384810399 19       316136857 1A
     32394244 1B          142544131 1C       611773546 1D
    245607503 1E          622689291 1F      1203374308 20 ( )
    445079752 21 (!)     3139879474 22 (")   425371380 23 (#)
    755116431 24 ($)      341914270 25 (%)  1261275093 26 (&)
    309100043 27 (')     2745227643 28 (()   257951963 29 ())
   6496479069 2A (*)      659103553 2B (+)   532192166 2C (,)
     58258531 2D (-)     1503042017 2E (.)   193549869 2F (/)
    621211728 30 (0)      332664326 31 (1)   341105086 32 (2)
     40049682 33 (3)      484745052 34 (4)   384356092 35 (5)
    339838758 36 (6)      269695295 37 (7)   629939645 38 (8)
    662273329 39 (9)     1931970178 3A (:)   554462692 3B (;)
    256567815 3C (<)      127356974 3D (=)   723511773 3E (>)
     89876226 3F (?)     1075689692 40 (@)  2564468584 41 (A)
```

```
     501077077 42  (B)      23940284 43  (C)    2199085762 44  (D)
    7174833205 45  (E)     468447150 46  (F)     525321380 47  (G)
     514900341 48  (H)     342301620 49  (I)      92671515 4A  (J)
     369042351 4C  (L)     935933960 4D  (M)     306710267 4E  (N)
     270457680 4F  (O)    2519734415 50  (P)    5220879305 51  (Q)
     694576708 52  (R)     304327143 53  (S)    5742277722 54  (T)
   15902439881 55  (U)    2662527484 56  (V)    5413326779 57  (W)
    1322661051 58  (X)    1100737359 59  (Y)     129542434 5A  (Z)
     480791190 5B  ([)    1530021825 5C  (\)    7580593143 5D  (])
     125280091 5E  (^)    2736642392 5F  (_)     391284075 60  (`)
     471678803 61  (a)     570428910 62  (b)     510275037 63  (c)
     431001136 64  (d)    1527591192 65  (e)     467204689 66  (f)
     649978745 67  (g)     168236427 68  (h)     330106136 69  (i)
    1669252908 6A  (j)     504412865 6B  (k)     312310323 6C  (l)
    1334447877 6D  (m)     628458562 6E  (n)     650643387 6F  (o)
     201598319 70  (p)     700486502 71  (q)      98911849 72  (r)
     499858133 73  (s)    1867137373 74  (t)    4814384784 75  (u)
     306552297 76  (v)    1612779465 77  (w)     831782596 78  (x)
      18823855 79  (y)     580914828 7A  (z)     280607036 7B  ({)
     706327468 7C  (|)    2714114344 7D  (})     526977663 7E  (~)
     487451765 7F         1138833221 80          123661648 81
    2824025341 82          366536954 83          586783131 84
     775622089 85          519799071 86          369869653 87
    2021511374 88          303480512 89         5137913138 8A
     604397234 8B          627901702 8C          111562168 8D
     925886169 8E          282622479 8F          341396319 90
     702225221 91          665553076 92          364695367 93
     613391059 94         2896648130 95          221080663 96
     458538263 97          943622380 98          253249947 99
    1237810204 9A          853985245 9B          118136042 9C
     438673928 9D          219524564 9E          864441999 9F
    2692981946 A0          537793289 A1         5134415487 A2
    1929572066 A3          145442015 A4          101105065 A5
    2658815638 A6         1092042075 A7         5525501549 A8
    2373521688 A9        15675573797 AA         4807653768 AB
     910170948 AC          643642842 AD         8112252534 AE
    2482283086 AF          611937552 B0          353668728 B1
     797046392 B2          468672035 B3          354417922 B4
     162005283 B5         1448814423 B6          260247203 B7
    1897761248 B8          565610846 B9         4149001951 BA
    2649507975 BB          658745041 BC          582514637 BD
    2899425384 BE         1210785600 BF          137666779 C0
     588924441 C1         1170989063 C2          249582141 C3
       6206616 C4          320465956 C5            3711355 C6
     420920780 C7          693138406 C8          252234844 C9
    1277320445 CA         1082146426 CB          469277288 CC
     316354609 CD          293601023 CE          266701551 CF
     837823715 D0          664558098 D1          118710652 D2
     117902695 D3          817645538 D4         6711103831 D5
     273212049 D6         2553366220 D7          245607503 D8
     290384750 D9          599774971 DA          464244527 DB
     565273595 DC         3115765667 DD          307057585 DE
    1476548390 DF          572663952 E0          165916208 E1
    1527506536 E2          490491845 E3          643155794 E4
     646911932 E5          410878308 E6         1324270449 E7
     465864602 E8          461042891 E9         4853812098 EA
    1631754935 EB          642433277 EC          978709913 ED
    3478808648 EE         1887422583 EF          300462826 F0
     740735879 F1          505204494 F2          923715959 F3
     707308466 F4         3294013483 F5          718558861 F6
     337574435 F7           79162893 F8          374143270 F9
    3709933092 FA         1853094643 FB          709152024 FC
    1527727186 FD          332543172 FE         1077855388 FF
Totals for non-ASCII sectors
summary format: <count> <hex value> <(actual character if printable)> ...
180157733376 00

500107862016 bytes, 976773168 sectors, 255 distinct values seen
624902595 sectors have printable text
```

Test Case FMP-04-DCO Image MASSter Solo-4 version 4.2.63.0		
	Runs of Sectors Unchanged or Overwritten First Sector Last Sector State 0 -- 976773167 Overwritten		

Results:	Assertion & Expected Result	Actual Result	
	FMP-AO-01 Hidden sectors overwritten	as expected	
	FMP-AO-02 Hidden area final state is	removed	
	FMP-AO-03 Visible sectors erased	as expected	
Analysis:	Expected results achieved		

4.2.15   FMP-04-DCO-HPA

Test Case FMP-04-DCO-HPA Image MASSter Solo-4 version 4.2.63.0	
Case Summary:	FMP-04. Overwrite hidden sectors using an ERASE command.
Assertions:	FMP-AO-01 If there is a hidden area present and the tool supports overwriting sectors contained in a hidden area, then all sectors contained in the hidden area shall be overwritten with the specified benign data. FMP-AO-02 A hidden area may optionally be removed from the storage device. FMP-AO-03 If the tool supports overwrite command selection and an ERASE command is selected then all visible sectors are overwritten.
Tester Name:	csr
Analysis host:	frank
Test host:	none
Test date:	Wed Sep 8 07:35:37 2010
Test drive:	26-LAP

Source Setup:	Size with DCO: 380721968 194.93 GB (10000000 sectors in DCO)
	Initial setup size: 365721968 from total of 365721968 (with 25000000 hidden)
	IDE disk: Model (TOSHIBA MK2049GSY) serial # (788DT0FLT)
	
	Sector 0 is first sector with printable text
	============= Start text =============
	00000/000/01 000000000000&&&&&&&&&&&&&&&&&&&&&&&&&&&&&&&&&&&&&&
	&&&&&&&&&&&&&&&&&&&&&&&&&&&&&&&&&&&&&&&&&&&&&&&&&&&&&&&&&&&&&&
	&&&&&&&&&&&&&&&&&&&&&&&&&&&&&&&&&&&&&&&&&&&&&&&&&&&&&&&&&&&&&&
	&&&&&&&&&&&&&&&&&&&&&&&&&&&&&&&&&&&&&&&&&&&&&&&&&&&&&&&&&&&&&&
	&&&&&&&&&&&&&&&&&&&&&&&&&&&&&&&&&&&&&&&&&&&&&&&&&&&&&&&&&&&&&&
	&&&&&&&&&&&&&&&&&&&&&&&&&&&&&&&&&&&&&&&&&&&&&&&&&&&&&&&&&&&&&&
	&&&&&&&&&&&&&&&&&&&&&&&&&&&&&&&&&&&&&&&&&&&&&&&&&&&&&&&&&&&&&&
	&&&&&&&&&&&&&&&&&&&&&&&&&&&&&&&&&&&&&&&&&&&&&&&&&&&&&&&&&&&&&&
	&&&&&&&&&&&&&&&&&&&&&&&&&
	============= End text Sector 0 =============
	9 <new line> characters inserted for readability
	
	Totals for all sectors
	summary format: <count> <hex value> <(actual character if printable)> ...
	  380721968 00 380721968 20 ( ) 185030876448 26 (&)
	  761443936 2F (/) 2196468178 30 (0) 1065666424 31 (1)
	  897239892 32 (2) 731585324 33 (3) 633593182 34 (4)
	  624635322 35 (5) 580892631 36 (6) 555053803 37 (7)
	  545751335 38 (8) 544997205 39 (9)
	Totals for non-ASCII sectors
	summary format: <count> <hex value> <(actual character if printable)> ...
	
	194929647616 bytes, 380721968 sectors, 14 distinct values seen
	380721968 sectors have printable text

Tool Settings:	Mode: Secure Erase Iteration: 1 Pattern: 00
Log Highlights:	Size after tool runs: 380721968 from total of 390721968 (with 10000000 hidden)

Test Case FMP-04-DCO-HPA Image MASSter Solo-4 version 4.2.63.0	
	Analysis of tool result --
	Sector 380721968 is first sector with printable text
	============= Start text =============
	23698/215/54 000380721968&&&&&&&&&&&&&&&&&&&&&&&&&&&&&&&&&
	&&&&&&&&&&&&&&&&&&&&&&&&&&&&&&&&&&&&&&&&&&&&&&&&&&&&&&&&&&
	&&&&&&&&&&&&&&&&&&&&&&&&&&&&&&&&&&&&&&&&&&&&&&&&&&&&&&&&&&
	&&&&&&&&&&&&&&&&&&&&&&&&&&&&&&&&&&&&&&&&&&&&&&&&&&&&&&&&&&
	&&&&&&&&&&&&&&&&&&&&&&&&&&&&&&&&&&&&&&&&&&&&&&&&&&&&&&&&&&
	&&&&&&&&&&&&&&&&&&&&&&&&&&&&&&&&&&&&&&&&&&&&&&&&&&&&&&&&&&
	&&&&&&&&&&&&&&&&&&&&&&&&&&&&&&&&&&&&&&&&&&&&&&&&&&&&&&&&&&
	&&&&&&&&&&&&&&&&&&&&&&&&&&&&&&&&&&&&&&&&&&&&&&&&&&&&&&&&&&
	&&&&&&&&&&&&&&&&&&&&&&&&&&&&&&
	============= End text Sector 380721968 =============
	9 <new line> characters inserted for readability
	Totals for all sectors
	summary format: <count> <hex value> <(actual character if printable)> ...
	194939647616 00 10000000 20 ( ) 4860000000 26 (&)
	20000000 2F (/) 49243664 30 (0) 19545258 31 (1)
	27640138 32 (2) 29035273 33 (3) 18858011 34 (4)
	13460565 35 (5) 12330523 36 (6) 13283567 37 (7)
	22563499 38 (8) 14039502 39 (9)
	Totals for non-ASCII sectors
	summary format: <count> <hex value> <(actual character if printable)> ...
	194929647616 00
	200049647616 bytes, 390721968 sectors, 14 distinct values seen
	10000000 sectors have printable text
	Runs of Sectors Unchanged or Overwritten
	First Sector Last Sector State
	0 -- 380721967 Overwritten
	380721968 -- 390721967 Unchanged

Results:	Assertion & Expected Result	Actual Result
	FMP-AO-01 Hidden sectors overwritten	DCO not erased
	FMP-AO-02 Hidden area final state is	resized (380721968 with 10000000 hidden)
	FMP-AO-03 Visible sectors erased	as expected
Analysis:	Expected results not achieved	

4.2.16   FMP-04-HPA

Test Case FMP-04-HPA Image MASSter Solo-4 version 4.2.63.0	
Case Summary:	FMP-04. Overwrite hidden sectors using an ERASE command.
Assertions:	FMP-AO-01 If there is a hidden area present and the tool supports overwriting sectors contained in a hidden area, then all sectors contained in the hidden area shall be overwritten with the specified benign data. FMP-AO-02 A hidden area may optionally be removed from the storage device. FMP-AO-03 If the tool supports overwrite command selection and an ERASE command is selected then all visible sectors are overwritten.
Tester Name:	csr
Analysis host:	frank
Test host:	none
Test date:	Fri Sep 3 12:55:48 2010
Test drive:	1C-SATA
Source Setup:	Size with HPA: 15000000 7.68 GB (219441648 sectors in HPA) Initial setup size: 15000000 from total of 234441648 (with 219441648 hidden) IDE disk: Model (WDC WD1200JD-00GBB0) serial # (WD-WMAES2049679) Sector 0 is first sector with printable text

Test Case FMP-04-HPA Image MASSter Solo-4 version 4.2.63.0	

	============= Start text =============
	00000/000/01 000000000000
	============= End text Sector 0 =============
	1 <new line> character inserted for readability
	
	Totals for all sectors
	summary format: <count> <hex value> <(actual character if printable)> ...
	  234441648 00 113938640928 1C 234441648 20 ( )
	  468883296 2F (/) 1461085523 30 (0) 678339301 31 (1)
	  497617498 32 (2) 407041791 33 (3) 391715334 34 (4)
	  376075228 35 (5) 347651457 36 (6) 332766225 37 (7)
	  332765657 38 (8) 332658242 39 (9)
	Totals for non-ASCII sectors
	summary format: <count> <hex value> <(actual character if printable)> ...
	
	120034123776 bytes, 234441648 sectors, 14 distinct values seen
	234441648 sectors have printable text

Tool Settings:	Mode: Secure Erase Iteration: 1 Pattern: 00

Log
Highlights:
	Size after tool runs: 234441648 from total of 234441648 (with 0 hidden)
	Analysis of tool result --
	Totals for all sectors
	summary format: <count> <hex value> <(actual character if printable)> ...
	120034123776 00
	Totals for non-ASCII sectors
	summary format: <count> <hex value> <(actual character if printable)> ...
	120034123776 00
	
	120034123776 bytes, 234441648 sectors, 1 distinct values seen
	No sectors have printable text
	
	   Runs of Sectors Unchanged or Overwritten
	First Sector Last Sector State
	      0 -- 234441647 Overwritten

Results:	Assertion & Expected Result	Actual Result
	FMP-AO-01 Hidden sectors overwritten	as expected
	FMP-AO-02 Hidden area final state is	removed
	FMP-AO-03 Visible sectors erased	as expected

Analysis:	Expected results achieved

4.2.17   FMP-05

Test Case FMP-05 Image MASSter Solo-4 version 4.2.63.0	
Case Summary:	FMP-05. Detect drive not supporting ERASE command.
Assertions:	FMP-AO-04 If an overwrite command is selected and the storage device does not support the command then the user is notified.
Tester Name:	csr
Analysis host:	frank
Test host:	none
Test date:	Wed Jul 28 15:40:35 2010
Test drive:	56-IDE
Log Highlights:	Message: Operation failed

Results:	Assertion & Expected Result	Actual Result
	FMP-AO-04 Selected command not supported	as expected

Analysis:	Expected results achieved

About the National Institute of Justice

A component of the Office of Justice Programs, NIJ is the research, development and evaluation agency of the U.S. Department of Justice. NIJ's mission is to advance scientific research, development and evaluation to enhance the administration of justice and public safety. NIJ's principal authorities are derived from the Omnibus Crime Control and Safe Streets Act of 1968, as amended (see 42 U.S.C. §§ 3721–3723).

The NIJ Director is appointed by the President and confirmed by the Senate. The Director establishes the Institute's objectives, guided by the priorities of the Office of Justice Programs, the U.S. Department of Justice, and the needs of the field. The Institute actively solicits the views of criminal justice and other professionals and researchers to inform its search for the knowledge and tools to guide policy and practice.

Strategic Goals

NIJ has seven strategic goals grouped into three categories:

Creating relevant knowledge and tools

1. Partner with state and local practitioners and policymakers to identify social science research and technology needs.
2. Create scientific, relevant, and reliable knowledge—with a particular emphasis on terrorism, violent crime, drugs and crime, cost-effectiveness, and community-based efforts—to enhance the administration of justice and public safety.
3. Develop affordable and effective tools and technologies to enhance the administration of justice and public safety.

Dissemination

4. Disseminate relevant knowledge and information to practitioners and policymakers in an understandable, timely and concise manner.
5. Act as an honest broker to identify the information, tools and technologies that respond to the needs of stakeholders.

Agency management

6. Practice fairness and openness in the research and development process.
7. Ensure professionalism, excellence, accountability, cost-effectiveness and integrity in the management and conduct of NIJ activities and programs.

Program Areas

In addressing these strategic challenges, the Institute is involved in the following program areas: crime control and prevention, including policing; drugs and crime; justice systems and offender behavior, including corrections; violence and victimization; communications and information technologies; critical incident response; investigative and forensic sciences, including DNA; less-than-lethal technologies; officer protection; education and training technologies; testing and standards; technology assistance to law enforcement and corrections agencies; field testing of promising programs; and international crime control.

In addition to sponsoring research and development and technology assistance, NIJ evaluates programs, policies, and technologies. NIJ communicates its research and evaluation findings through conferences and print and electronic media.

To find out more about the National Institute of Justice, please visit:

www.nij.gov

or contact:

National Criminal Justice
 Reference Service
P.O. Box 6000
Rockville, MD 20849–6000
800–851–3420
http://www.ncjrs.gov